THE WILD PARTY
VOCAL SELECTIONS

MUSIC AND LYRICS BY **MICHAEL JOHN LaCHIUS**

Produced by
Alfred Music Publishing Co., Inc.
P.O. Box 10003
Van Nuys, CA 91410-0003
alfred.com

Printed in USA.

ISBN-10: 0-7390-6352-9
ISBN-13: 978-0-7390-6352-1

Cover Photos
[Illustration]: [Miguel Covarrubias (Used by Permission)] • [Poster Design]: [Paula Scher/Pentagram]

MICHAEL JOHN LaCHIUSA

Michael John LaChiusa—composer, lyricist, and librettist—established himself as a powerful presence on the American musical theatre scene after winning Off-Broadway's 1993 Obie Award for his musicals *First Lady Suite* and *Hello Again*. He was represented on Broadway in the 1999–2000 season by two more musicals, *The Wild Party* and *Marie Christine*, which together received 12 Tony Award nominations.

LaChiusa's full-length musicals *See What I Wanna See*, *Bernarda Alba*, *Little Fish*, *The Highest Yellow*, *Hello Again*, *First Lady Suite*, and *The Petrified Prince* have had their original productions presented by preeminent theatre companies across the U.S. and internationally. In 2009, his musical *Giant*, based on Edna Ferber's novel, with a libretto by Sybille Pearson, premiered to resounding acclaim at the Signature Theatre in Arlington, Virginia. In addition to cast albums that are available for most of his musicals, his songs have been recorded on solo albums by artists ranging from Lea DeLaria to Audra McDonald, and can be heard on McDonald's best-selling debut album, *Way Back to Paradise*, among many others.

Mr. LaChiusa has contributed articles to the *New York Times* and other periodicals, and was an adjunct professor at Yale School of Drama. He is currently on faculty at New York University and is a guest lecturer on musical theatre at universities across the U.S.

Photo: Waring Abbott

GEORGE C. WOLFE

In addition to *The Wild Party*, George C. Wolfe's directing credits for the theatre include *Jelly's Last Jam* (Drama Desk and Outer Critics Award), *Angels in America—Millennium Approaches* (Tony and Drama Desk Award), and *Perestroika* (Drama Desk Award), *Bring in 'da Noise, Bring in 'da Funk* (Tony and Drama League Awards), *Topdog/Underdog* (Obie Award), *Twilight: Los Angeles 1992* (Drama Desk Award), *Elaine Stritch at Liberty* (Tony Award: Unique Theatrical Event), *The Tempest*, and *Caroline, or Change*, which won the Evening Standard and Oliver Awards for Best Musical.

Mr. Wolfe directed the films *Nights in Rodanthe* and *Lakawanna Blues*, for which he earned the Directors Guild Award, a National Board of Review Award, an Independent Spirit Nomination for Best First Feature, a Christopher Award, and the Humanitas Prize. *Lackawanna Blues* won four NAACP Image Awards, earned seven Emmy Award nominations, and premiered at the Sundance Film Festival.

Mr. Wolfe is the writer of the award-winning *The Colored Museum*, which he also directed for PBS. He also adapted and directed *Spunk* (Obie Award) and created *Harlem Song* for the world famous Apollo Theatre. From 1993–2005 he was the Producer of the Public Theatre/New York Shakespeare Festival and was named a living landmark by the New York Landmarks Conservancy.

Photo: Julia Maloof

CONTENTS

QUEENIE WAZZA BLONDE

Music and Lyrics by
MICHAEL JOHN LaCHIUSA
Based on the text by
Joseph Moncure March

Raunchy

(Percussion)

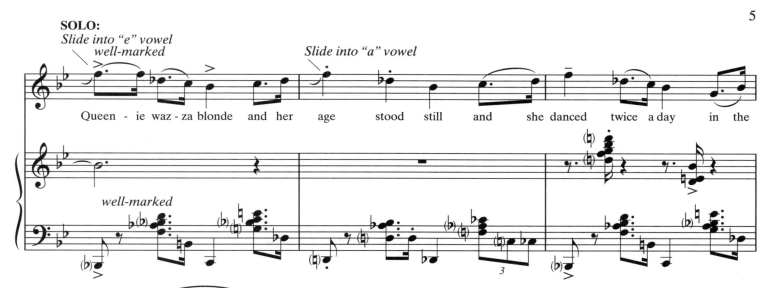

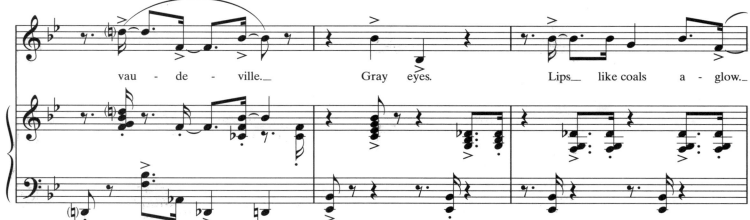

MEN:

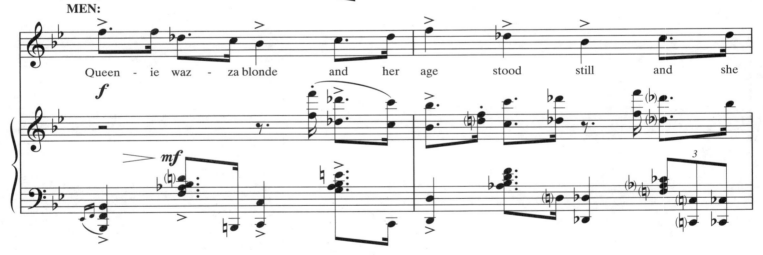

Queen - ie waz - za blonde and her age stood still and she

danced twice a day in the vau - de - ville._ What hips.

What shoul-ders.__ What a back__ she had.__ Her

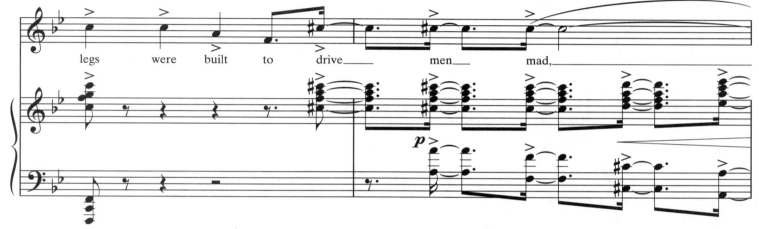

legs were built to drive__ men__ mad,__

fast

faster Rock it

mad,__ mad,__

faster **ff** Rock it

8

mad.

Presto

A tempo
WOMEN:
(A)'rri-ver - dac - ci

QUEENIE:

A - pa - la - chee!

Woo!

(dry) Wooo.

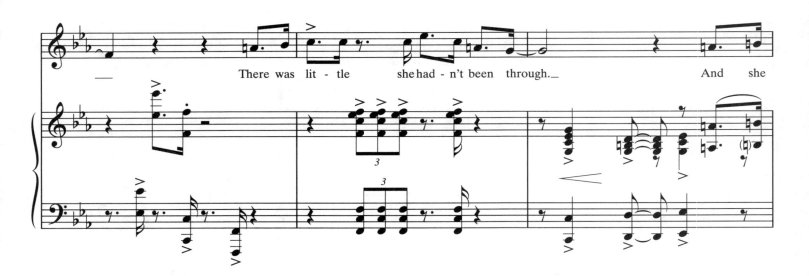

There was lit - tle she had - n't been through.___ And she

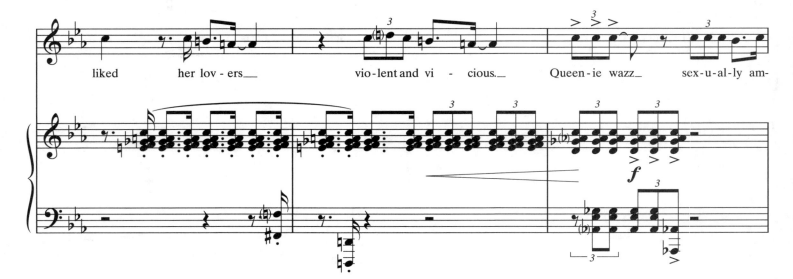

liked her lov - ers___ vio - lent and vi - cious.___ Queen - ie wazz___ sex - u - al - ly am-

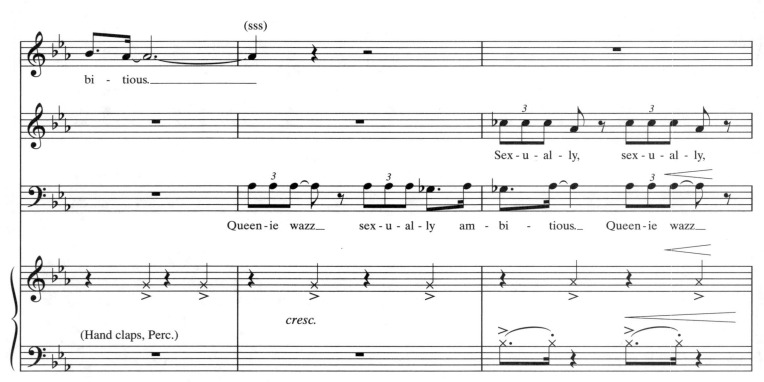

bi - tious.___

(sss)

Sex - u - al - ly, sex - u - al - ly,

Queen - ie wazz___ sex - u - al - ly am - bi - tious.___ Queen - ie wazz___

(Hand claps, Perc.)

cresc.

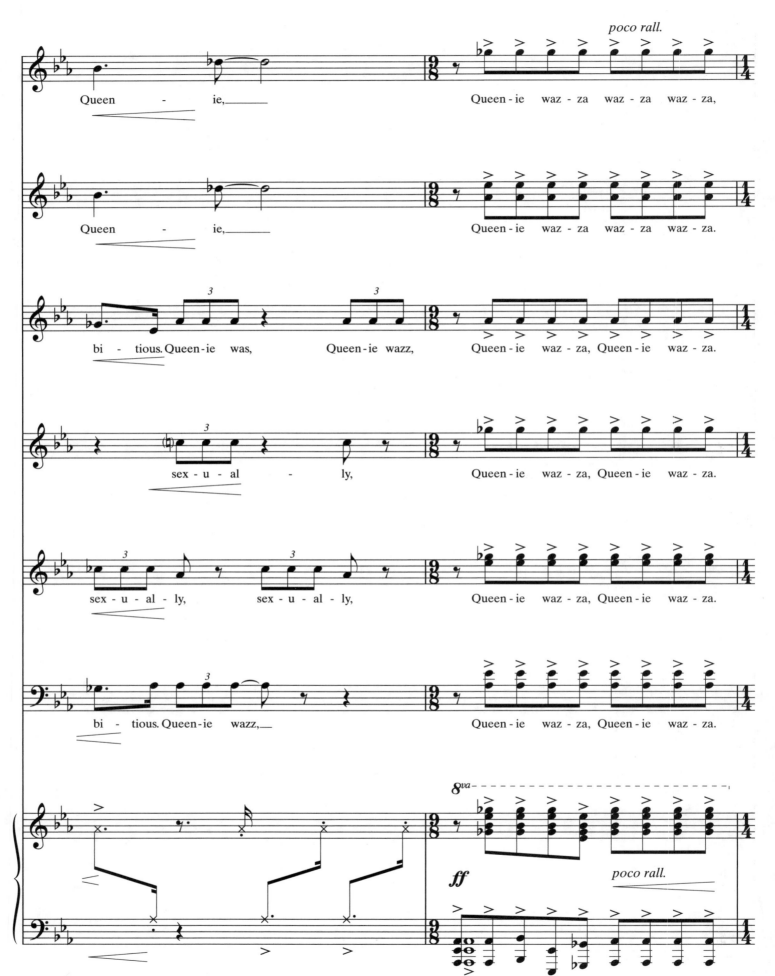

Queen-ie!

waz - za waz - za   waz - za waz - za   Queen-ie!

waz - za waz - za   waz - za waz - za   Queen-ie!

ie waz - za,   Queen - ie waz - za,   Queen - ie waz - za   Queen-ie!

Queen - ie waz - za waz - za waz - za, Queen - ie waz - za, Queen-ie waz - za   Queen-ie!

Queen - ie waz - za waz - za waz - za, Queen-ie waz - za, Queen-ie waz - za   Queen-ie!

cresc.   molto cresc.   loco

(8vb)

WILD PARTY

Music and Lyrics by
MICHAEL JOHN LaCHIUSA

Slow, sinuous

BURRS:

I think we're due to have a big___ par - ty. The time is ripe to toss a

huge___ she - bang. Say me and you, we throw a wild par - ty.

We'll round up all the old gang.___ 'Cuz, ba - by, we're

too steamed,__ and we need to get cooled out.__ We need to get

QUEENIE:

Aw - right.

strung__ tight.__ We need to get some - thin' soon, aw - right? You

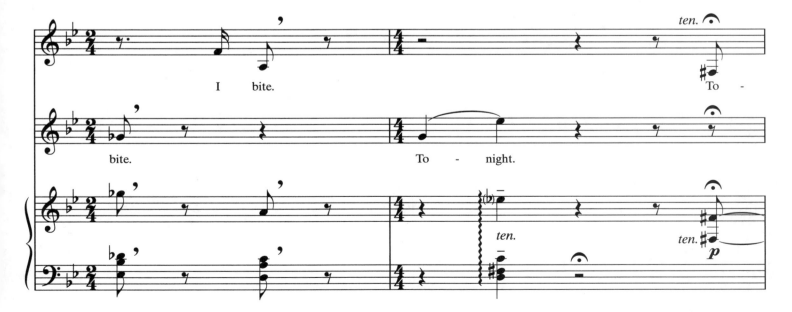

I bite. To -

bite. To - night.

Fast, hot, urgent

night…

Put out the news we got a hot___ par - ty. Put out the word 'n' go 'n' or - der the ice.

We sure could use a lit - tle fun, lov - er. When was the last time___ I wore my "new" strap - less?

When was the last time___ you smiled?___ When was the last time___ we had a real par - ty?

Wet and wick-ed fast-time fun and___ wild.___

QUEENIE:
You're the clown. *You* fig-ure it

BURRS:
Whad-d'-ya mean by "fun"?

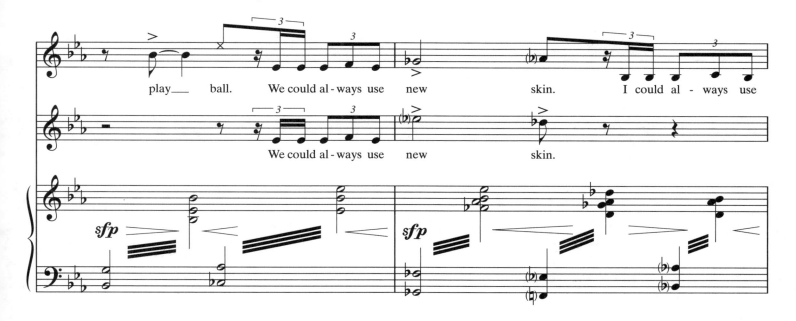

play___ ball. We could al-ways use new skin. I could al-ways use

We could al-ways use new skin.

poco rall.

some-one fresh and tan and thin. You in?

We're out-ta gin. I'm___ in.

f poco rall. *p colla voce*

p pull back *attaca*

Broadly

B:

Go fix your face, we got-ta get___ read-y.

f *p* *f*

Pick out the mu - sic that you wan - na hear._____

Q:
colla voce
Let's give this place a lit - tle life, lov - er.

B:
Let's give this place a lit - tle life, lov - er.

colla voce

mp

hold

Q:
colla voce
When was the last time__ I danced the black bot - tom?

B:
You're not get-ting an - y young-er, my child.

colla voce

legato

Fast

When was the last time_ we had a real par - ty? Last year, last month, yes - ter-day, but

When was the last time_ we had a real par - ty? Last year, last month, yes - ter-day, but

one that - 'll nev - er be as_____ wild,_____ wild._____

one that - 'll nev - er be as_____ wild,_____ wild._____

WELCOME TO MY PARTY

Music and Lyrics by
MICHAEL JOHN LaChIUSA

Hot boogie-allegro

QUEENIE:

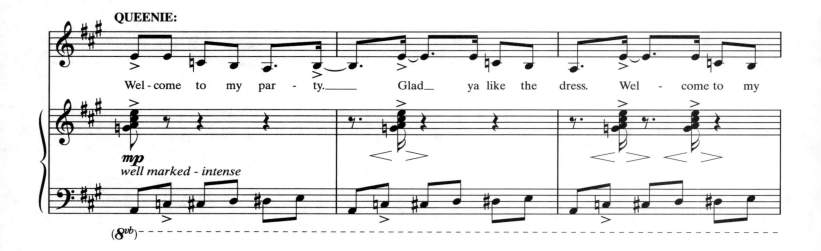

Wel - come to my par - ty.___ Glad___ ya like the dress. Wel - come to my

mp
well marked - intense

par - ty.___ (Ba - by, where's my ice?___) Who___ here's up for ac - tion?___

Welcome to My Party - 7 - 1
33566

Who__ here's_ new?_____ Wel-come to my par - ty.__

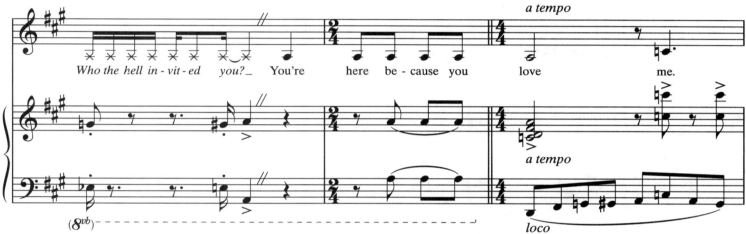

Who the hell in - vit - ed you?_ You're here be - cause you love me.

Don't I know it? Yes, I know____ you're here____ be-cause you

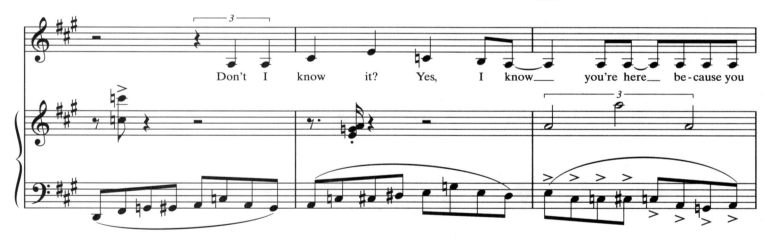

love____ me, and 'cuz the booze is cheap and the

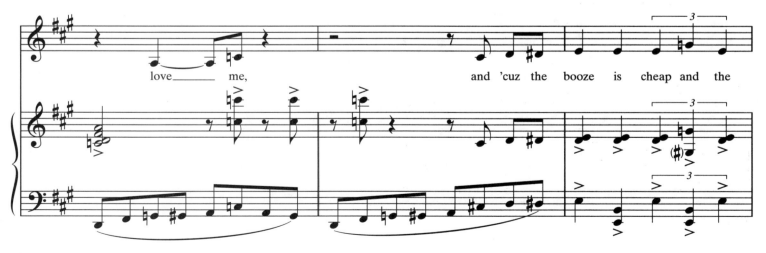

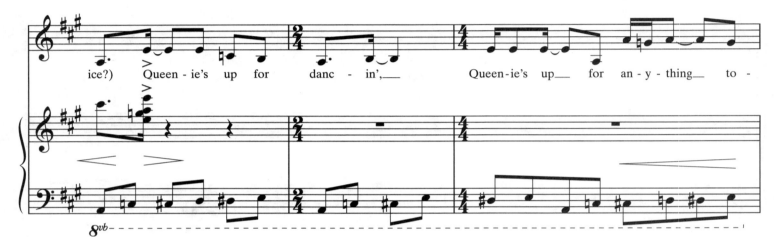

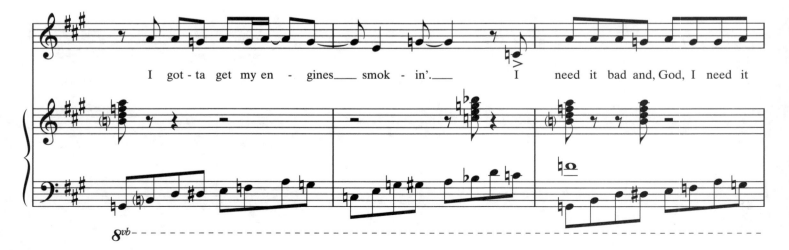

more. I need a lot - ta friend - ly strok - ing. There

ain't no heav-en and there ain't no hell, no turn-ing back, Dad - dy, lock the door.

Wel - come!

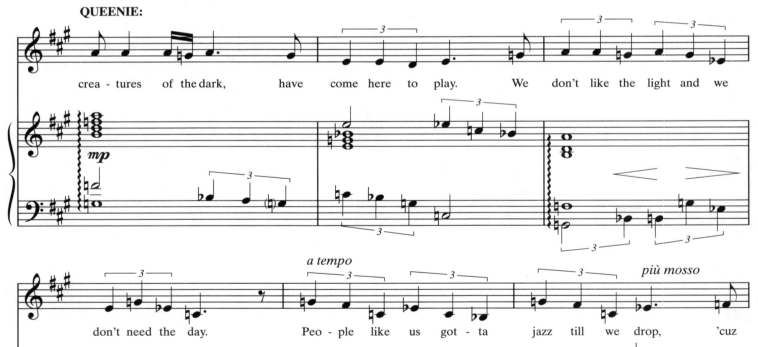

QUEENIE:

crea - tures of the dark, have come here to play. We don't like the light and we

a tempo *più mosso*

don't need the day. Peo - ple like us got - ta jazz till we drop, 'cuz

peo - ple like us, we don't know when to stop.___

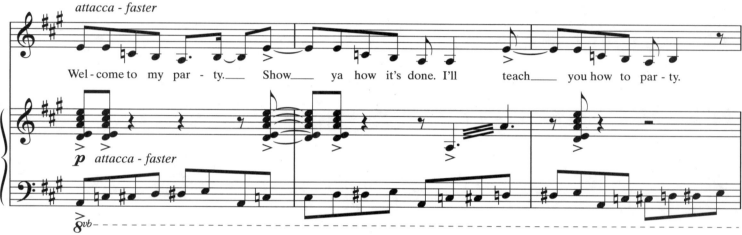

Wel - come to my par - ty.___ Show___ ya how it's done. I'll teach___ you how to par - ty.

(Where the hell's___ my ice?!___) You'll re - mem - ber this one.___

Queen - ie's guar - an - tee.___ Wel - come to my par - ty.

UPTOWN

Music and Lyrics by
MICHAEL JOHN LaCHIUSA

Uptown - 8 - 1
33566

day._____ The rest of the world____ may be

lynch - ing and kill - ing and dy - ing, so what? C'est la

vie! Man - hat - tan's a bub - ble of re -

ju - ve - nat - ing jazz - in'. Who cares a - bout the rest of the world?_

LOWDOWN-DOWN

Music and Lyrics by
MICHAEL JOHN LaCHIUSA

Moderate blues

QUEENIE:

Some are born for high - er things.

Like hitch - in' up to up - town kings. I was born for

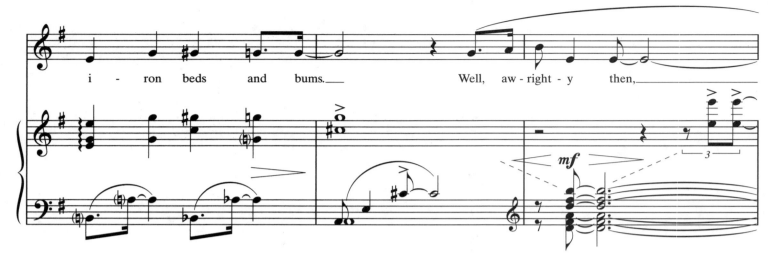

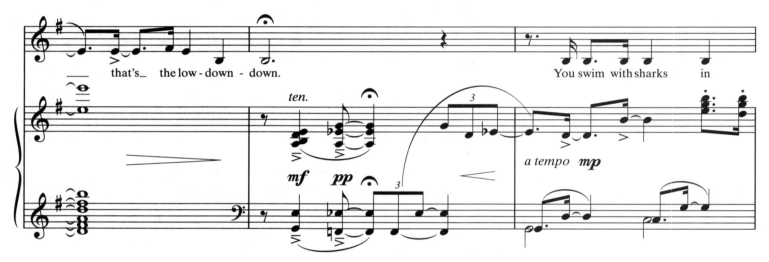

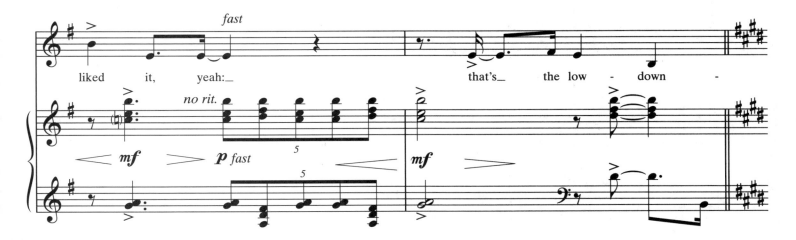

liked it, yeah:__ that's__ the low - down -

down.

Some get good at traf - fick-in' in souls.

I got good at roll - in' with the rolls.

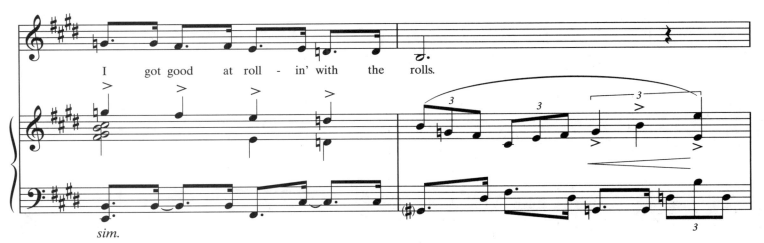

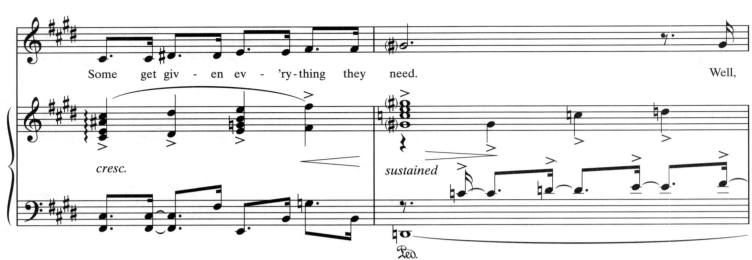

Some get giv - en ev - 'ry-thing they need.   Well,

cresc.   *sustained*

that's a luck - y break.   I steal what I can take and I roll,___

poco accel.

and I plead,___   and I duck,___

poco accel.

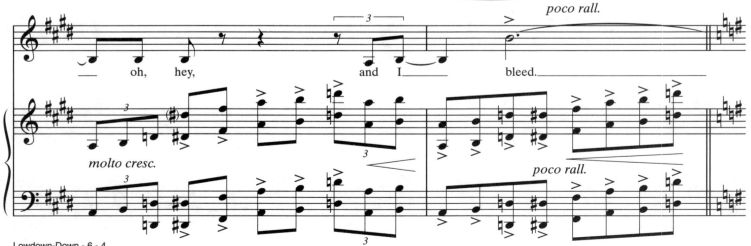

poco rall.

___ oh, hey,   and I___ bleed.___

molto cresc.   *poco rall.*

Some are born to rise___ a - bove___

sleep - less___ nights and___ sloe gin___ love (love)

(love). I___ was born to ask "Why_ was___ I born?" And the

an - swer is...___ *"Get me some ice, will ya?"*

BLACK IS A MOOCHER

Music and Lyrics by
MICHAEL JOHN LaCHIUSA

Moderato - lowdown, sensual

KATE:

Black is a mooch-er and I like it like that.___ Three___

___ pock-et pooch-er and I like it like that.___ I like him the way that he

Lyrics:

hm mm - hm mm - hm,___ I like it like... In the morn-ing light,___ when he

rubs his beard, then he touch-es me.___ In the af-ter-noon,___ when he

draws my bath, then un-dress-es me.___ Come 'round cur-tain time,___ when he

spends my dough, then he cheats on me.___ Come the quar-ter moon,___ when he

mp più mosso

cresc.

f

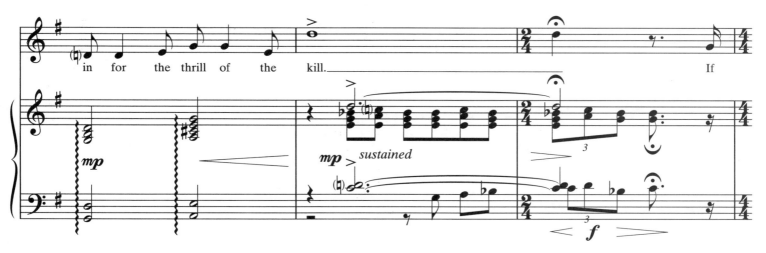

in for the thrill of the kill._____ If

I can't have him,_____ then no-bod-y

will. Uh-huh uh-huh uh-huh uh-huh, I like it like this. Mm-

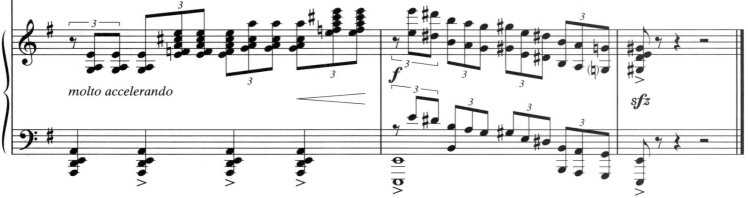

hm mm-hm mm-hm, I like it like___ Black._____

PEOPLE LIKE US

Music and Lyrics by
MICHAEL JOHN LaCHIUSA

BLACK:

Peo-ple like us, we get by through the day, sur-viv-in' the cit-y way bet - ter than most. We

go through the mo - tions___ from night-cap to night-cap, here but not here with the heart of a ghost.

People Like Us - 8 - 1
33566

Peo-ple like us, we meet__ up some night in a room full of strang - ers who__ call them-selves friends.__

__ It feels__ like a dream,__ but it's too__ hard to tell where the dream__ be - gins__ and the real world ends, and

poco cresc.

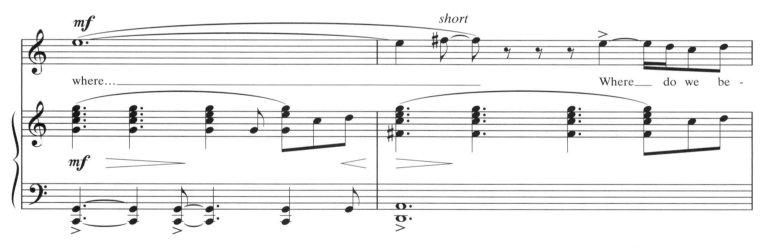

mf   short

where..._____ Where__ do we be -

mf

long?   We might have to ask our - selves:_____ Where?_____

mf

Where do we be - long? Peo - ple like us,

pri - vate stock. Where?

QUEENIE:

Peo - ple like us, we take lov - ers like pills, just hop - in' to cure__ what we know__ we can't fix.__

__ And we'll lay__ in their arms and we'll say__ pret - ty things; we'll be there but not there, but we'll still__ get our kicks.__

AFTER MIDNIGHT DIES

Music and Lyrics by
MICHAEL JOHN LaCHIUSA

Lento, sempre legato

ain't so hard to_____ see_____ the truth. No

need for lies. What we are is all we are_____ af - ter

mid - night dies._____

After Midnight Dies - 2 - 2
33566

GOLDEN BOY

Music and Lyrics by
MICHAEL JOHN LaCHIUSA

Moderato - graceful waltz

Golden Boy goes down, hell, the crowd, they get mean, can't believe what they've seen, can't be true. When the

Golden Boy - 6 - 1
33566

white boys_____ string you up._____ Don't think you

won't._____ When the Gold - en

Boy goes down,_____ it should make you a he - ro._____

EDDIE:

It don't.

When the Gold - en

Boy goes down,_____ he drops flat on the mat and you

think, "Well, that's that," but whoa no._____ When the

Gold - en Boy goes down,_____ fame steps up with a

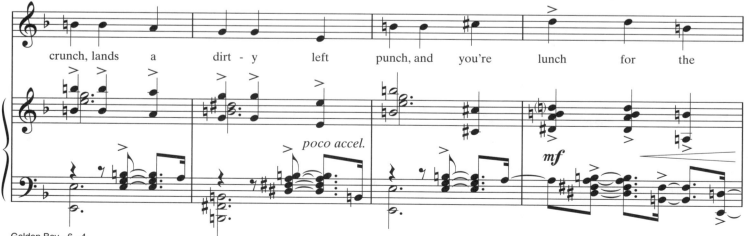

crunch, lands a dirt - y left punch, and you're lunch for the

64

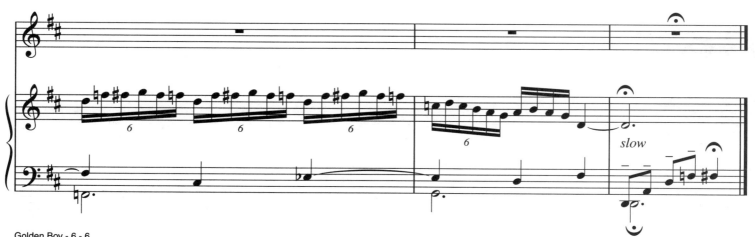

HOW MANY WOMEN IN THE WORLD?

Music and Lyrics by
MICHAEL JOHN LaCHIUSA

How Many Women in the World? - 8 - 1
33566

Lyrics:

How man-y wom-en on the earth? How_ man-y wom-en can I bear? How_ come I put up with that_ one who's tan-gled in my hair._ She's got in me ev-'ry-where, in my skin, in my blood, all I hear and see. How man-y wom-en on the earth get in so deep, they kill my sleep? How man-y man-y man-y man-y man-y man-y man-y

a tempo

wom - en?_____ She._____

What oth - er wom - an would like the punch - es? *POW!*_____

What oth - er wom - an would like the punch - es? *POW! POW! POW!*

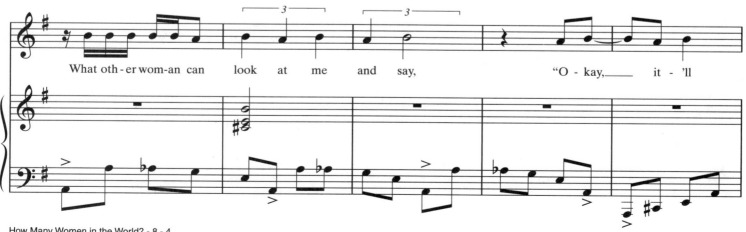

What oth - er wom - an can look at me and say, "O - kay,_____ it - 'll

accelerando poco a poco

do"?_____ "O - kay,_____ it - 'll do"?_____

accelerando poco a poco

mp

"O - kay,_____ it - 'll do"?_____

molto cresc.

più legato

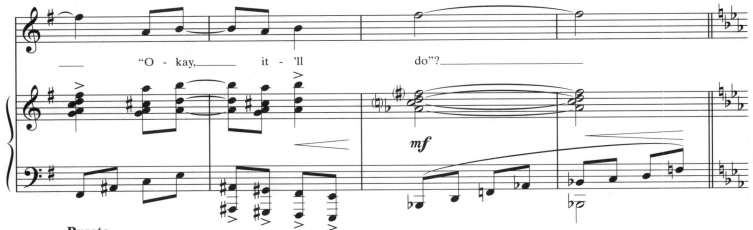

"O - kay,_____ it - 'll do"?_____

mf

Presto

"Ma - rie is trick - y, sly and stick - y. Brud -

f

da, you watch out for that gal._____ She gon - na love ya like there's

molto rit.

no to - mor - row,_____ but come to - mor-row, you got plen - ty of

molto rit. f

tempo primo

sor - row."_____ O - kay,_____ it - 'll

tempo primo p pp

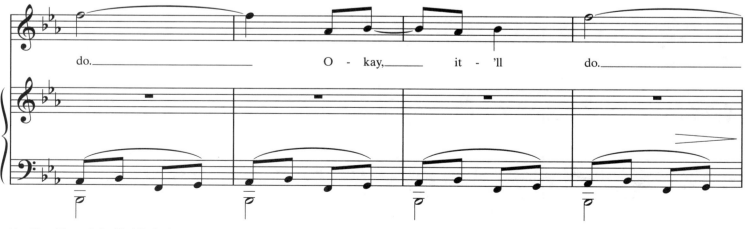

do._____ O - kay,_____ it - 'll do._____

How man-y wom-en in the

world? How__ man-y wom-en can I take? How__ much more of

that one can I take be-fore I break? But I'm not gon-na

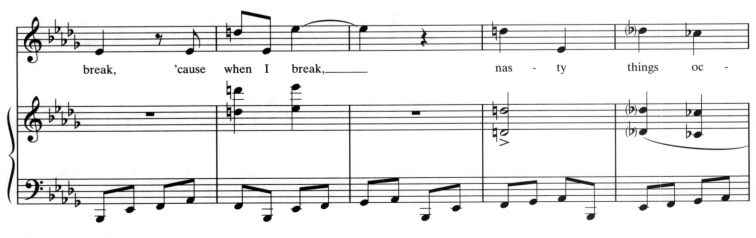

break, 'cause when I break,__ nas - ty things oc -

WHEN IT ENDS

Music and Lyrics by
MICHAEL JOHN LaCHIUSA

Moderato

DOLORES:

So you think the par - ty's gon - na last for - ev - er. And you'll

al - ways fly this high, but that de - pends. The high - er the high, the hard - er you're gon - na

When It Ends - 5 - 1
33566

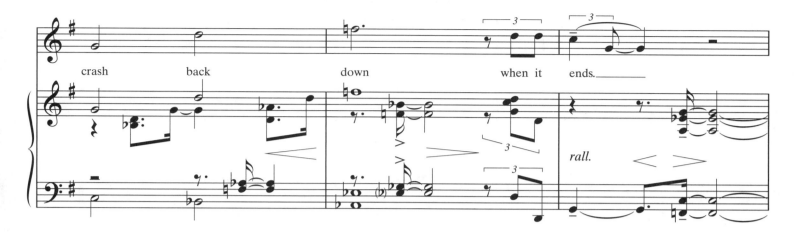

crash   back   down   when it   ends._____

rall.

You   can   make   a   for - tune   do - in' next to   noth - in'._____   You   can

a tempo

sit   there   on   your   ass   and   screw   your   friends.   But   you   bet - ter know how   to

mf

kick,   kick,   kick your way out   of   the   burn   -   ing

l'istesso, sharply accented

mf

room   when it   ends.   You can

sell your bod - y to the high - est bid - der.   You   can   call it love and cash the div - i -

dends.   You can take a mil - lion lov - ers, but you're on   your

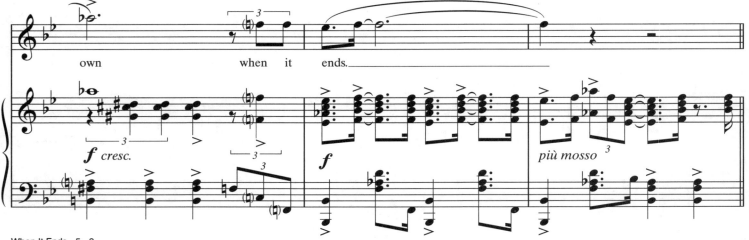

own   when it   ends.

When It Ends - 5 - 3
33566

bet - ter hope to Je - sus or Mo - ham - med or *what - ev - er*

that you got the right stuff_____ when it

ends._____ When it ends._____

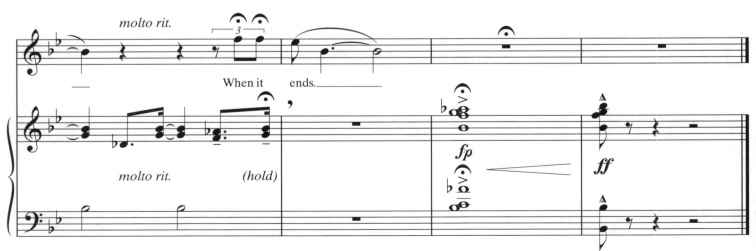

When it ends._____

THIS IS WHAT IT IS

Music and Lyrics by
MICHAEL JOHN LaCHIUSA

This Is What It Is - 5 - 1
33566

This Is What It Is - 5 - 5
33566